City Safari

Fox

Isabel Thomas

Raintree

Raintree is an imprint of Capstone Global Library Limited, a company incorporated in England and Wales having its registered office at 7 Pilgrim Street, London, EC4V 6LB – Registered company number: 6695582

www.raintreepublishers.co.uk
myorders@raintreepublishers.co.uk

Text © Capstone Global Library Limited 2014
First published in hardback in 2014
The moral rights of the proprietor have been asserted.

Edited by Dan Nunn, Rebecca Rissman, and Helen Cox Cannons
Designed by Tim Bond
Original illustrations © Capstone Global Library Ltd 2014
Picture research by Mica Brancic
Production by Helen McCreath
Originated by Capstone Global Library Ltd
Printed and bound in China

ISBN 978 1 406 27127 0
17 16 15 14 13
10 9 8 7 6 5 4 3 2 1

British Library Cataloguing in Publication Data
A full catalogue record for this book is available from the British Library.

Acknowledgements
We would like to thank the following for permission to reproduce photographs: Alamy p. 23 den (© blickwinkel/S Gerth); FLPA pp. 4 (Panda Photo), 10 (Roger Tidman), 13 (Phil McLean), 16 (Terry Whittaker), 20 (Jurgen & Christine Sohns), 23 earth (Jurgen & Christine Sohns), 23 scavenge (Panda Photo); Getty Images pp. 8 (Jim Dyson), 11 (Oli Scarff), 18 (David Strydom), 23 mate (David Strydom), 23 senses (Oli Scarff); Naturepl.com pp. 5 (Geslin/© Wild Wonders of Europe), 6 (© David Kjaer), 7 (2020VISION/© Terry Whittaker), 9 main (© Andy Rouse), 9 inset (© David Tipling), 12 (© Fabrice Cahez), 14 (© Laurent Geslin), 15 (Geslin/© Wild Wonders of Europe), 17 (2020VISION/© Bertie Gregory), 19 (Laurent Geslin), 21 (© Fabrice Cahez), 23 territory (Laurent Geslin; Shutterstock p. 23 roadkill (© Valeniker).
Front cover photograph of a fox reproduced with permission of Shutterstock (© Keith Livingston); back photograph of a fox in a shed reproduced with permission of FLPA.

We would like to thank Michael Bright for his invaluable help in the preparation of this book.

Every effort has been made to contact copyright holders of material reproduced in this book. Any omissions will be rectified in subsequent printings if notice is given to the publisher.

Warning!

Never touch wild animals or their homes. Some wild animals carry diseases. Scared animals may bite or scratch you. Never hold food for a fox to eat. It may bite your finger by mistake.

Note about spotter icon

Your eyes, ears, and nose can tell you if a fox is nearby. Look for these clues as you read the book, and find out more on page 22.

Contents

Some words are shown in bold, **like this**.
You can find them in the glossary on page 23.

Who has been caught raiding the rubbish bin?

Red-brown fur. Pointed ears. A bushy tail. It's a fox!

You don't need to go to the countryside to spot wild animals.

body a bit bigger than a pet cat

pointed ears

red-brown fur

long, thin nose

black legs

Thousands of foxes live in cities and towns.

Come on a city safari and find out if foxes are living near you.

Why do foxes live in towns and cities?

Foxes live where they can find food, water, and shelter.

It's easy to find food where people live, and cities are warmer than the countryside.

You might spot foxes on golf courses and in parks.

But their favourite city homes are big, messy gardens.

What makes foxes good at living in towns and cities?

Foxes can see, hear, and smell very well.

Their **senses** help them to find food, even in the dark.

8

Foxes can run faster than a human sprinter and jump the height of a door.

These skills help them to escape from danger quickly.

Where do foxes hide?

Foxes make **dens** in hedges, compost heaps, under sheds, and on roofs.

They like to hide from people during the day.

Look out for foxes just before dawn and just after dusk.

This is when they come out of their hiding places to find food.

What do foxes eat?

Foxes hunt small animals, such as rats, moles, birds, and insects.

They also eat food that they find, such as fruit and **roadkill**.

The area where a fox looks for food is called its **territory**.

Foxes leave signs such as droppings to warn other foxes to keep out!

Why do foxes like to live near people?

Foxes sniff out food in bins, rubbish tips, and on the streets.

Some people even put food out so that they can watch foxes in their gardens.

4

City foxes do not need to hunt as often as countryside foxes.

People throw away a lot of food, so foxes often find more than they can eat.

What dangers do foxes face in towns and cities?

hen house

Not everyone likes living near foxes.

Some people hunt or trap foxes to stop them damaging gardens, or stealing pet chickens or ducks.

The biggest danger to city foxes is crossing the road.

Cars kill most city and town foxes before they are two years old.

Do foxes live alone?

Foxes live in family groups, but they like to hunt and feed on their own.

Every winter, pairs of foxes get together to **mate**.

Foxes make lots of noise at this time of year.

Male foxes may fight to keep other males out of their **territory**.

How do fox cubs learn to live in towns and cities?

Fox cubs are born in spring, in special **dens** called **earths**.

The whole family helps to look after the cubs.

Fox cubs love to chase, play-fight, and chew everything they find.

Playing helps them learn how to hunt and **scavenge** for food.

Fox spotter's guide

1. Foxes have four toes on each foot. They leave diamond-shaped footprints with claw marks.

2. Foxes have special eyes that work well in the dark. This makes their eyes shine in bright light, such as car headlights. They may be the first thing you spot!

3. When foxes eat animals, their droppings are full of bone, fur, and feathers! They have a pointy twist at one end.

4. Foxes like to bury spare food to eat later. Look for signs of digging in flowerbeds and flowerpots!

5. Listen out for fox calls, especially in winter. Male fox calls sound like three short barks. Female fox calls sound like screams.

Picture glossary

den hidden home of a wild animal

earth special fox den, where babies are born and looked after

mate when a male and female animal get together to have babies

roadkill dead animals that have been killed crossing roads

scavenge look for food that has been thrown away or left over

senses sight, hearing, smell, taste, touch

territory area that an animal lives in, and defends from other animals

Find out more

Books

The RHS Wildlife Garden, Martyn Cox (Dorling Kindersley, 2009)

Wild Town, Mike Dilger (A & C Black, 2012)

Websites

www.foxforest.com/upclose/voicescarry.shtml
Listen to different fox calls on this website.

www.thefoxwebsite.org
Find out more about foxes on this website.

Index